THE ALWAYS BROKEN PLATES OF MOUNTAINS

THE ALWAYS BROKEN PLATES OF MOUNTAINS

Rose McLarney

Four Way Books
Tribeca

Copyright © 2012 by Rose McLarney
No part of this book may be used or reproduced in any manner
without written permission except in the case of brief quotations
embodied in critical articles and reviews.

Please direct all inquiries to:
Editorial Office
Four Way Books
POB 535, Village Station
New York, NY 10014
www.fourwaybooks.com

Library of Congress Cataloging-in-Publication Data

McLarney, Rose, 1982-
 The always broken plates of mountains / Rose McLarney.
   p. cm.
 ISBN 978-1-935536-19-2 (pbk. : alk. paper)
 I. Title.
 PS3613.C5725A59 2012
 811'.6--dc22

2011027993

This book is manufactured in the United States of America
and printed on acid-free paper.

Four Way Books is a not-for-profit literary press. We are grateful for the assistance
we receive from individual donors, public arts agencies, and private foundations.

This publication is made possible with public funds
from the National Endowment for the Arts

and from the New York State Council on the Arts, a state agency.

Distributed by University Press of New England
One Court Street, Lebanon, NH 03766

[clmp] We are a proud member
of the Council of Literary Magazines and Presses.

Contents

Gather   3
Don't I Know   4
Living Up   5
Domestic   6
At the Mountain State Fair   7
Salvage   8
Autumn Again   10
Builder and Keeper   11
Parallel Cuts   14
The Dance   16
A Reproach   17
Appetite   18
Flock   19
Double Yolk   20
Simply Put   22
In Admiration   23
Poet   24
Shadow Shape   25
Negative   26
Untruss   27
Where I Will Live   29
Before Me   30
    1. Settled this Hollow
    2. Worked this Farm
    3. Survived this Loneliness

Disclaimer   38
Our Stories   41
About Farming   43
Drought and Divorce   44
Young Couple   45
Femenino   46
Heart   47
Shiner   48
Jubilation, Then   50
The Drive Home   51
We're Not Much for Words, But   53
Covenant   54
First Bruise, First Feast   56
They Said It Was Too Late   57
Three Wishes   58
Ars Poetica   59
By Immersion   61
Longer Still   62
Little Fish   64
Flourish   66
Desire   67
I Learn to Be Still, Like the One I Love   69
Epilogue   70

For my mother and father

Gather

Some springs, apples bloom too soon.
The trees have grown here for a hundred years, and are still quick
to trust that the frost has finished. Some springs,
pink petals turn black. Those summers, the orchards are empty
and quiet. No reason for the bees to come.

Other summers, red apples beat hearty in the trees, golden apples
glow in sheer skin. Their weight breaks branches,
the ground rolls with apples, and you fall in fruit.

You could say, *I have been foolish*. You could say, *I have been fooled*.
You could say, *Some years, there are apples*.

Don't I Know

A man who was not to be trusted
once owned the hound. Don't I know

the kind. But I won't walk the way
the stray dog does,

head down, side-stepping, skitter.
He's pulled taut, fear hauling against

his troublesome tendency
towards faithfulness.

Yes, he runs the ridges and feeds himself.
His feet are fast, his teeth sharp.

But what I watch is how he stops to pluck
sweet blackberries.

Hound on the hill,
sun-warm fruit in the hound.

There is a tenderness that persists.
When he bays above us,

a longing song, let me turn
to take a new man's arm.

Living Up

The ceilings are five feet high, house crowded
by history and rotting rafters he'll have to tear out—
the tall, young man who just bought it.
Beside a stooped old apple
(too long un-pruned to be bowed by fruit),
while the day backs down
behind the ridge, he makes plans.
He wonders, for a moment, what it would have been
like to be born here, though he is hearing
the answer when peepers in the boggy place below
send up their little staggered songs
and let them fall down. If you have had
spring evenings, then you know
how it has always been here: Love always shot
with the feeling this is the last of it.
Always told to outgrow
the mountains that would block your view,
these serious, sad playhouses, these low, old places
where you want to hunker, where you can't
stand up straight.

Domestic

The sows are in heat, squealing and pink.
The wild boar comes from the forest
to batter at their pen.

I go out and smash the ice
on the trough. The water
breaks free. This takes
a pick ax. Wielding it, I feel wild.

But the only strength in this story
is the fences'. Not even boars are wild—
imported for hunting a hundred years ago,
crossing the sea in a rich man's crate.

When I hang up the pick ax
it freezes to the nail, clinging as I do,
making my living elsewhere and

returning to farms after sunset,
the barns symbols
just discernable in the dark.

At the Mountain State Fair

That'll do,
the herdsman calls
to his collies,
but they are deaf to him.

Rides are lighting up the night,
shaking people and making them shriek.

It does not matter that the dogs
could not do their work.
There was no crowd.

Animals and flowers
are not what they come for
anymore.

If he stood beneath
the Ferris wheel saying *Away,*

it would listen.
Turning, turning from him.

Salvage

After they clear-cut his family land
to put in the interstate,

the timber was left to lie and rot.
So he restores the tools his great-grandfather

used, harvesting a few trees
that were ancient even then.

He clamps the saws—rip saws,
coping saws—to steady them,

and sharpens. He mills the wood,
cuts it to length, and assembles it.

He twists pegs out of a scrap, pounds
them into screw holes, knocks the excess off,

and sands it all smooth.
Then layers on a dozen coats of finish.

When the table is dry,
he sits pots on it, straight from the stove.

No hint of the heat shows
in his thick polish,

and he says nothing against change,
or about missing that deep, familiar shade.

Autumn Again

The hills, stabbed with sumac,
maple. I know
the color is beautiful but
this time of year, there is always
a wounded feeling.
You are working in the kitchen
and explain that when one piece of trim
is cut to cover the raw end of another,
it is called a *true return*.
I want to weep, as if I had ever left
or done you any wrong.

Builder and Keeper

A rough framer, her love
sets sturdy king and queen posts. He takes care
with cripple rafters and bird's-mouth notches too.
Evenings afterward, she feeds him
fittingly, equal parts strength and sweet,
bread, dough rested and risen, and angel food,
beaten and overturned. And matches
his work, its words, in her way,
decorating the table with golden saxifrages,
the smallest flowers whose name means
splitter of stone.

■

Pointed and circling, his fingers signal
the crane to raise and lower
the glass up to where it is indefinable
against the sky, then into a wall where it is window.
Her fingers pick an unidentified plant
with five petals, five sepals, five stamens.
It's not cumin, coriander, caraway,
can't be eaten. But it's of the carrot family
so protects what grows beside it from pests—
a *companion plant.*
He will cross his arms to stop the machines.
She will curl her fingers, *Come to me.*

▪

His hands make right angles,
roofs' rises and runs.
She holds her finger and thumb up
to the moon to tell its phase.
It's waning when the crescent
sits in her left hand, waxing
when it fits her right. By moonlight,
she lays one hand on the left side of his chest—
his heart. The other flings back out of bed,
open—measure of the width she waxes.

▪

Nut around bolt. Rail run through stile.
Mortice cut in timber, tenon enters.
Molding coped in the corner, one piece shaped
to cover the other. Hammer held
by belt loop. Belts and sashes entangled
in the dresser. Teacups in each other's laps.
Nesting mixing bowl set. Sprout coiled inside seed.
Wet flower petals pasted transparent, tight
against tree trunk. Hips between thighs.

Curve of his chest against her back, knees notched
together. Good night
dovetailed into the next day.

■

When he arrives at the job site first, he just sits
in the quiet before saw, sander, and drill.
Turkeys call their mates. Branches remember
the boards, touch tips to scaffolding.
He pulls her long hair from his beard and lets it drift.
This is not idleness. Birds collect the strands,
work them into their nests; a house is being built.

Parallel Cuts

The door front is made of quartersawn wood,
the back from plainsawn
to save expense.

One is screwed
to the other.

The quartersawn, cut at angles from the log,
wastes great
amounts of wood

to yield
pieces of certain grain.

The plainsawn, cut across the growth rings,
leaves no scraps.

Heat rises and the door warps.
Wood drinks water from air,

as when its fibers were connected,
circulating through a thing still living.
The door swells in its sill,

oak board buckling
as a whole weeping willow bows.

The builder, unable to open the door,
wishes, of course, for better wood,

but also
wood equally weak.

The back is gaping, pulled apart
from the front,
groaning its own way.

All plainsawn
suffers the same—
fetal or stooped, however frail—

it curls together.

The Dance

Sunday, there's a sale
on the bypass, folding tables
set up on the highway's weedy margin.

Men already wearing camouflage
only blend into the tigerstripe and treebark
they buy, forest patterns irrelevant

against the traffic. Today,
they are hunters. They seek
coats, and cover.

Monday, builders again, they paint over
fingerprints and measurements on walls
immaculate as if created by no man.

One moves a sheet of plate glass alone,
his grip all against its great
shivering, bowing ability to break.

Seen from a distance, he dances
empty-handed.

A Reproach

The blade fills the span of his arms,
or that's how it looks.
Using both hands, his whole body, he bows
and pulls the tool through
the side of beef, from top to bottom.
All day, as skinned carcasses
pass down the line, he makes this one movement.
At dusk, he steps out of his uniform, the blood,
and though the machines start again at dawn,
a reason remains
for him to hurry away, straightening his collar
with a stroking touch, a fondness for the living
still in his hands.

Appetite

There's a new owner of the old
tobacco farm down the road.
Now he raises buffalo—
for lean meat.

But the buffalos' great shapes
cannot move in the spaces between mountains.
They cut the slopes with their hooves,
cloud the creeks, kill the pasture.

So he buys hay,
thousands of rolls a season.
It's easier to leave the barn doors open
than to move the hay out every morning.

So he lets them eat as much as they will.
They stab their horns in the hay
and toss it over their shoulders in celebration.
They cover themselves in gold and bellow.
They burrow into the hay.

Days later, he finds bulls
suffocated under the bales.
Such bodies, buried
by blades of grass.

Flock

He had big plans, bought a thousand
chickens. But when one moves
to the corner to get out of a draft,
all the others follow, in a crushing pile.
Though he throws running birds back
against a tide of beaks and clawed feet,
in the end, he's knee-high
in bodies. A hundred dead,
each time the wind blows.

Passing his place before, I had believed
the amble of outbuildings
across the land, added over the years,
spoke of steadiness.
But what's behind others' walls isn't any better.
Every bird in the flock
feels the same desperation.

Still, if I went down and found him,
the sight might seem beautiful:
white feathers falling from the air
and covering a man.

Double Yolk

Looking for fractures,
you bent at a conveyor belt, moving
eggs over a light, one after another—
illuminated, illuminated.
Through the dirtied shells you could see
life growing. It was ours,
a common one, another love story,
told with the force
of the flock's thousand voices.

■

You left early, the syrup smell
of breakfast barely covering sleep's smell.
Yet always returned,
never wearing strange perfume,
but barn scent—the odor of working,
towards a ring, in a ring, back to me—
and, shitted to your shoes,
feathers. Angel,
I admire chickens, flightless
and faithful.

■

It was the year of double yolks.
You worked an extra job, packing produce,
brought home the eggs that were too big
for standard cartons, and saved to buy diamonds.
You gave me a two-ring set,
and because we were innocent—we were—
and didn't know one was for engagement, the other
for marriage, I began to wear both at once.
The rings were white gold, the yolks were bright gold,
every morning I opened a shell, and out slipped
an excess of richness.

Simply Put

As we back out,
the cattle trailer swings around
and shatters the truck window.

The cattleman says,
*I hate to see a thing like that happen
to anybody,*

a statement as encompassing
as the way the window broke—
the whole, reduced.

Such wide goodwill,
and still, we drive away, pieces
of glass falling behind.

They look like common jewels,
or I say that as the wind beats us,
so we don't have to speak

of what the lovely
leaves incomplete.

In Admiration

Goats press together,
guarding bellies.

This is a herd's agreement:
to be nothing

distinctive
and let wolf, dog, any other

save them from deciding
which will be sacrificed.

So they stand always
beside each other,

heads bowed—
heads with horns

and still, they bow.

Poet

I don't know what the donkey sees
standing in the pasture where he's been
longer than I've been alive, most of the time
with his head down. (Some soft light
between the blades?) Or the chickens,
who feed by digging into the dirt,
walking backward. But I do know what
the dog who sleeps on the side of the road
doesn't see. He has watched countless cars
going elsewhere. Now he has cataracts, and squints
at moving things, as I do when I want to understand
and wonder, *Symbol? Metaphor?*

Shadow Shape

Geese pass, their shadow shape
a point.

They honk so they won't stray
from formation.

They call out to say, *I am here,*
just behind you.

It is not a lonely sound.
Do not look for loneliness,

a hard pit for every center.
Even when they land they are light,

dusting their wings,
sending the dust into the air and sun,

so dust gleams.

Negative

When the calf dies, he buries it
with the tractor. He is sorry,
but there are vultures.
Afterward, the mother
bellows at the tractor,
suspicious of the steel bucket
that brings her hay.

And I think most of how I love him
when I sleep alone, and lie awake,
imagining how tractors overturn,
and animals are angered—
what could keep him away.

What's most noted are the cold body,
the cold machine, and the place left empty,
though the field is daily filled
with a herd of thousand-pound animals
seeking shade from the sun under willows
and steaming in the rain.

Untruss

Look for them in long-standing buildings,
the ends of I-beams.

When the cattle market is turned to condos,
it's divided into dozens of spaces, each

with their own load-bearing walls. The steel
that spanned it all is removed, leaving

a stub embedded in plaster or, where a beam was
pulled out, the indentation of its absence.

Even with the I gone,
structures stand.

And we still stand
in them. But it's only bodies

between walls, under roofs with
fingers' clicks on keyboards our steps and song.

Our selves have left.
They soften in the rain,

draw up into the black places
we saw in the overlap of leaves

against the light,
filter through the shifting spaces

between poplars we walked into,
the axis of each trunk

giving over to grove.

Where I Will Live

An old man joins me as I study the barn,
wormy chestnut gone gray. The sun sets

behind it. Boards alternate with absences,
railings against the light cast at us.

A barn wall makes way for a boulder
at its corner, each board cut to length

and curved to fit. It must accommodate
the flux of rock.

*So people could try to grow
on the good land,* he says, *they built*

in the hardest places.
I bought the farm. I'm moving in

to the house, beyond the barn,
on stonier ground. He's come to help me

feel at home.

Before Me

1. Settled this Hollow

It is rumored that, in the past, high iron content in the region's spring water caused psychosis in women.

Iron is their answer. The men
lay iron track and drive iron spikes,
to hold the railroad to the mountainsides,
to hold a way out, open.
My husband breaks rock with metal.
Another man follows, replacing the rock with metal.
But the iron only fights back a mile of the forest a day.

An iron pan—you have to handle it carefully.
I remember this, though I don't bother
with cornbread anymore. I eat jelly by the spoonful.
When he comes home, my husband serves himself
the meat we had smoked for winter.

Use soap on your skillet or scrub too hard, and the metal
will flake away in soft pieces. I've been taking note
of softening things: the slow splitting
of the lintel above the canning house door,
and how the roof is folding, preparing to go with it.
The rocks that let go of the hill
and fall heavily, burying themselves in the fields.

The way the last apples
in the cellar keep some shape,
but brown and sag, rotting from the inside.

I see the same color that bloomed on my skillet
crusting the rocks where the spring water backs up.
That water's brighter than the orange of jewelweed.
Summer afternoons, I've started crouching in the cool
of the weeds. When you press them,
the jewelweed pods come undone,
drawing back and flinging the seeds away. My husband
holds his hands stiffly at his side when he speaks to me now,
trying to keep calm, I think.

I can't seem to care about the chores. I left
the white enamel basin, filled with wash water,
on the porch a week ago. Now the inside's burnt orange,
like the spring. This morning, I thought I'd clean it, but
I stumbled again. The basin bouncing down
the stairs chimed in time with the bells
ringing in my head.

When the winter comes,
and the leaves and all the living things
know it's time to go,
and I'm snowed in alone—

I think I'll be glad for color in the water then.
I can see sitting by the spring, only the water moving
enough not to freeze, against acres of white,
bright as blood.

There's no lack of water here.
There's even water in the air, in clouds of mist
that start to circle me when I stare at the sky.
Springs ooze out from under every rock.
I used to think this was the rock's apology
for hiding the soil where we could have grown something.
But I tried many springs, and each had the strange taste,
like licking a knife.

My husband, hunched from laying track, talks of progress.
The train will transport rubies, or mica.
They'll build mines. They'll build schools.
The missionaries have renamed Devil's Fork;
they're calling it Sweet Water.
I can't believe him, that they'll make a road over
those peaks. I stay here in the hollow,
surrounded by slopes. Always, there's the sound
of springs, water that can only come down.

2. Worked this Farm

I don't understand why the cows bellow so
when we take the calves—don't they want
to be left alone? I can't get enough time to myself.
Even if no one's here, there's the headstones
in the plot on the ridge, looking down.
We pass on family names, so somebody
with any name you know is up there already.
It's true, I don't have much company—
my sisters got married, each gone off
to live, and sleep, and always be with one man—
but that's what lets father watch me so close.

Except when we make ice cream, and everyone
sits around in a rapture, slipping spoons
in and out of their mouths.
It's not the sweetness I like—
it's all the neighbors, and nobody
paying me mind. If there is fiddling after,
we are all sinning, so I dance. And sometimes
I pick a man and fix my eyes on him,
all those lessons about steadiness of hand and heart
at work in my look. Then, in that crowd,
I know I'm the only one
he sees. To tell you the truth, I'm drawn to heat.

I'd like to stay outside until the summer soaks my dress.
But they send me to the milking parlor again.
I press myself against the copper pipes
that run through the creek to chill,
I try to appreciate the cool, I think on
how everyone hates milk when it turns bad.
When my sisters visit, I'm to join them
in the shade under the trees, breaking beans,
making every one into two.
The blind gentian, a pretty blue flower
that never opens, blooms there.

3. Survived this Loneliness

Honey

Running through the forest
with his hatchet,
it's sweetness he's seeking.

He'll follow a bee all day,
go straight through the brambles,
stop each time it settles
on a flower, until it leads him
to the hive. I remember
how persistent he could be,
how patient.

Then he'll cut into the tree
and honey will run out.
When he took me
with him, I watched and thought
he could get to the gold
inside anything.

Once he chased me.
Now, he claims hives,
carving only his own initials
into the bark.

Sorghum

I wanted sweetness—
that's what drew me to him.
But I've learned to earn it
in better ways.
When people harvest
their sorghum cane, I'll come
stoke the fire and stir the juice.

While I work, they say nothing
about shame.
I'm happy to stand by
that boiling vat all day
for the chance
to skim off the impurities' foam.

The juice thickens. It gets harder
to move the paddle through.
But I do, pushing toward the time
when it's finished, when the syrup
will be clear.

Cider

My daughter has the same
weakness. That's why
I like cider best before it turns hard.

It's not that I can talk
of resisting temptation.
But now I can only
feed the stomach's hunger.

I add the fresh-pressed apple
to batter for sweetness.

I show her what little
shape shifting I can do:

Take the pan out of the fire
and turn it over.
The liquids and loose
powders become a cake,
and it stands, on its own.

Disclaimer

Every Sunday, I climb the mountain
to a rock outcropping
called Lover's Leap.

People say it's named for a Cherokee girl
who threw herself off
to her death, out of love
for a man from an enemy tribe.

The records, however, mention only
a coon hunter.

He stumbled over the rock
and survived his injuries.
I'm sure he hurt,

but you can see why they tell the story
the way they do,
and why I prefer their stories.

■

After questions such as, *Did he love me,*
Did I love him enough?

long walks and more distant histories
become attractive.

In history, there are facts,
and there are disputed facts,

and it is bearable to consider either answer.

■

So I look down on the little town from the rock,
and pick out recognizable parts:

the house where we once lived,
the old school

where class was taught *blab style*,
children repeating lessons aloud together.

It's the talk of people past
I continue,

though I am an inexact student, unfaithful
to the details.

I think they would forgive me

for what I do with words,
like a new girl, who can only
sign her name with an X.

Our Stories

"The kingdom of heaven is to be taken by violence or not at all."
—Flannery O'Connor

*You are so beautiful it's harmful
to a man*, he said as they sat on the steps
of a stilled mill at the foot of the Blue
Ridge, dynamite blasted red.

When he skipped church as a child,
a dog bit off his ear. He carried it
to the hospital out of sight in its own box,
seeing and hearing the evil of loss.

While he carried wood,
a piece of the pillar of his spine slipped
and the means of making fire
flew from his arms.

Hit by a car walking home, his collar
bone broke, set him free from the hold
of his chest. In the workshop, his hands
split. The bones gave up the flesh.

Much has fled men like him. His are stories
to stay away from. So she comes
close, like the sun *down south*, so called,
down to the damage where she is home.

We are so harmed we are beautiful:
the buildings abandoned by paint,
the now unfarmed fields, the always
broken plates of mountains.

About Farming

It's hard however you do it. But you could choose
to cultivate flowers. They bloom delicate
under glass in big greenhouses, whole valleys glowing
with their fear of the dark. You could produce
tomatoes, so suddenly plentiful, the hot fruit
falls and fills paths all through the bottomland,
and bursts between your barefoot toes,
until the blight, for a summer month or so.
What I did was go up on High Lonesome
to raise evergreens. After all, men most love the women
who turn away, or maybe the ones they never know,
the flash of a bright dress, rounding a corner,
the pale leg through a skirt slit, in sight, then out—
and I came to understand that. I chose
a place where the land turned north. What I grow wants
the cold to come; it's only after the freeze
that the trees can keep their needles,
no matter how you shake them.

Drought and Divorce

Bare shoulders,
        no rain on them.

Endless sun
        and no hay to make.

Every day has been fair.
        The cattle will be butchered.

Dry creek beds will run
        beef-blood red.

It will be a winter of eating steak,
        hateful work of the husbandman.

Young Couple

They walk through a construction site,
and over a bridge,

just poured.
He tells her about concrete:

how Romans kept it from cracking
by mixing in blood,

and the way that it hardens,
giving off warmth.

She kneels to feel it.
The heat, their bodies—

that's what they thought of then.
And even the future.

They should have also noted
the arch of the bridge,

that it was a vacant space
bearing the weight.

Femenino

No is all Gerardo and I say the same way.
The deep voice of rain drowns mine, trying
to explain how the posts should be set,
wire stretched. My arms are spread
to show distance. (How far we are,
from the house of my marriage, the mesh
of its fences, though they kept
little in the end. And Gerardo's home country—)
Or spread in the gesture of beseeching.
Then salvation is a muddy truck. A friend pulls up
as the sky clears (compliant symbol). He
knows no Spanish, uses the same words I have,
but firmly so Gerardo somehow understands,
so the work is done.

When they've all gone, how will I
make the best of it? The bear skin I found
in the barn, force the hardening leather
around my shoulders, wear it through the woods?
Better to get a kitten to illustrate blind bravery,
stumbling softly through the spring grass
on feet it has not yet grown to fit.
Already, again, the knuckled clouds
swing at the sunset. It risked,
briefly, being pink.

Heart

As a test, pull the lips up, press
the gums pale, then release.
A healthy goat's vessels refill,
the color, the blood, rush back.

Trim the hooves to stand level,
cut back edges, dirt, hard dark
to white, but stop before pink,
blood in tissue showing through.

If I'd been so aware, of blood,
what moved it, outside my fences,
watched for flushing, listened
for men's skipped heart beats,

then goats' eyes turned to mine,
the weight when I hold them,
all a ribcage contains and
the warmth it can release,

wouldn't be so staggering.
This beating would bring me
to my knees, if I weren't
already kneeling in the hay.

Shiner

When the creeks were full,
we were

going fishing, and you
said, *I'd like to come home to a house*

with fish on a stringer
and you inside.

∎

But now there's a drought here, dust.
Not even poison ivy shines.

And you call a city home.
Streams creep under you

unknown in culverts.
Do you notice

if the soil's dry, study
the cloud's intimations?

∎

They say your neighbor's dogs bark all night
and you get up to hose them down.

I've asked about you.
I think of you with water in your hands.

I understand why catch come
to a shiner lure, imagining

you under the streetlight,
and how the spray must sparkle.

Jubilation, Then

Once, stories,
what a drunk said—
I want only two things in my house:
a piano and gas lamps,
for courting purposes, you understand—

were like explosions of elderberries
arrayed on stems, pawpaws' leather
swelling with creamy meat.

I collected them as if they had value,
picking fruit, picking flesh.

The Drive Home

One is hungry and so we share in her want,
all of the women peeling away from the bar.
Among the many and the clink of glasses
toasting each other—and chairs and corners,
everything the crowd presses them to touch—a voice
is calling after us, *It's cold out there. Come cozy up to me.*
But we go, to a café, and there we understand the belly dancer,
how she wants to be loved. So she chooses our table to seduce,
confiding in us with lips pursed, then parted, an eyebrow arched.
Each shake that takes her body away to the left is undone
by the one that brings it back to the right. Watching her
unfurled stomach, rich hips in sequined, fuchsia silk,
those of us who have said we had no appetite
consider filling ourselves with grape leaves, lamb, Turkish delight.
The woman beside me whispers, *I like how that
has no function as either a sleeve or a glove*, speaking of satin
around the dancer's arm, above the wrist and baring her shoulder.
Outside, it is cold and we clump together, cutting through
line cooks speaking Spanish, circled around
the fire of cigarettes, stopping when we understand
they are offering us one, continuing until we come to the theater.
There will be a show, and actors pretending so they can make real
feelings in us, our possible tears won with their spit in the spotlight,
so close it glows, and then the drive home. For me,
it is a long one, and because I do not sing, I slap myself
to stay awake, traveling through country where lights grow lesser
and the houses keep greater and greater spaces between each other.

At dawn, dry-mouthed and disliking the light, another long drive
anywhere, for groceries and more gas. I pass horses on a steep slope
standing apart in what looks like an argument for being alone forever
because love is when the track of your talk comes undone
and you spill your stories into each other and these animals are still,
breathing fog but certain, certain of singularity, this morning.
This is country for the ones who have stayed
true to self-sufficiency and silence
and speak of *family land, kin, our kind, where you come from,*
and will not come too close to you, when they do speak,
or when walking by. (They'll never cross your land.)
After the horses, there's a house on fire, but I only see the smoke
and a scattering of onlookers, a man I might have married standing
back at a safe distance.

We're Not Much for Words, But

Blackberries,
suspended in moonshine,

enlarged with alcohol,
skins stretched taut,
almost to bursting

and preserved, sit on the shelf.
They wait, purple and potent,

with the promise that, if we drink,
our skins will press together,
and our lips will split
in speech.

Covenant

In Latin America, I never spoke. I understood
what I heard, I knew some words. But never the right ones,

and restraint was all I had to distinguish myself.
I was pale while the purple-black custard flowers

smelled so strongly insects mistook them for carrion,
men rippled by, their muscle mounted on horses' muscle,

and there was such music and dancing.
It is like that here now, when I walk past bars, the men

on the sidewalks, slight hips tilted,
holding in their hands scotches, cigarettes,

symbols of pleasure—
I find so little language for the ways men are beautiful.

They are not meant to be admired like women;
we can afford only occasional attractions.

And if I have studied men's similar shirts, made out
the shoulder blades, inferred from the forearms,

that should cease soon.
I will marry one, and say to many,

Look how I can love, how I could have loved you.
The way I love this one is how you should all be loved.

I'll choose a love, as I choose my home,
an old white farmhouse, not far from where I grew up.

I'll choose a temperate climate, trees with reasonable leaves,
and the familiar brown sparrows in their branches, fully

remembering the rainforest's damp heat, Resplendent Quetzals
in the twisted vines, the cries of tropical birds.

First Bruise, First Feast

The bride beckons her bridesmaids
to climb the silo,
and they do,
hoopskirt wire ringing
against the ladder,
lining the steel tower
with fuchsia, powder pink, red, and orange satin.

She is above the dancers
who lifted the groom to their shoulders
and have stumbled and dropped him,
and the bluebird that flew
against a window and flaps circles under the peonies
with its remaining wing.

What does she expect of their life?
Shading her eyes, she is also looking past
the ease of an early summer evening,

guests taking slices of both cakes;
beneath the tables, puppies
boneless in their utter sleep;
children and kittens streaking across the field
ahead of dusk,
arms and tails canted at what must be the angle
of aimless pleasure.

They Said It Was Too Late

They said it was too late. They said
it had passed: the time
when you could make a living
with your hands. But I met a man
who told the kind of stories
I wanted to hear—like how
he picked corn in the morning,
frozen tassels cutting his face
and the sun out of sight,
finding the ripe heads by feel,
seeking out those soft
to the touch—
and wrapped his fingers
around mine in the dark.
He even talks of being early,
and bright light. About a farmer
who cut his hay green, went on
and baled it, and put it in the barn.
It steamed in the tight rolls
and burst into flame.
The place is still smoking.

Three Wishes

To have two long-legged dogs
named Thither and Yon,
loyal to me. A man
who hears when I say, *Let me alone,*
and lifts me over fences and creeks
anyway. And an understanding
of the moss that lines paths
through the woods, if it
invites me onward, or
to lay down where I already am.

Ars Poetica

I wouldn't settle for so little space, get so close,
    sitting in the middle of a truck's bench seat,
        legs spread to accommodate the gear shift, his hand on it.

But I am in the rearview, watching you,
    wishing my way into that empty passenger seat,

        where I could study the woman's face,
        how she chooses
what to cleave to.

Neither would I keep myself more apart,
    chaining a barking dog by my door,

who runs the same old circle, and
wears away the ground to be crossed over.

You say I turned out different,
    but we sat in the same school together all those years,

        while chalk mining weighted the air with dust,
        so though we were young,
we breathed as if disturbing an abandoned place.

We all watched erasure
        as the mountain dropped lower,
        went white, and then left only

        the black board of the stormy sky,
the new, dark blank before us.

So I'd think you'd understand—I thought
        writing would be

no more likely wiped away than anything else here
        I could have cared for.

By Immersion

To get a pure pumpkin,
one with sweet, smooth flesh, you had to
pollinate by hand and tape the blossom
closed. Otherwise, the plants would cross,
get fertilized by any squash around.

Black horses wouldn't stop rolling
in dust, in ecstasy,
legs up and out from under every load,
until their intestines tangled.
Or, at least that's what was said in warning,

like they said Hellbenders,
two-foot-long, slime-covered salamanders
that filled the river, were evil.
Hellbenders breathed through loose skins,
filtering that water for decades,

and I swam in it, I went in deep.

Longer Still

Sundays in summer,
a young girl swims in the river,
floating the swiftest part,
where the Cherokee built a fish trap,
two stone walls converging
in a V. Fish had funneled down
the rapids into the narrowing space
to be netted, and now
her body follows their path,
caught again and again.

The other children are in church,
learning that at sea somewhere,
Jonah had been eaten by a whale,
and they must obey.
The girl's parents love her, and let her
run wild, and she chooses to stay home.
She swims alone, though
she has heard the legend
about a giant fish in this river
who swallowed warriors whole.

She wouldn't mind being swallowed.
And she holds her breath under water,
for a long time, and longer still, until
her limbs drift away and she is aware
of only the current roaring around her.
She wants to stay there forever.

If she had, she later thinks, looking back
at her life, the people
she has listened to and tried to love,
there would have been little lost.

Little Fish

    Fishermen want brook trout,
      those big temperamental beauties

who died off when the water got cloudy.

At dawn now, you can look downstream
and there won't be a single human silhouette,
      wading in or casting out.

But the creek is still alive

with fish, with the dozens of small species
      we cannot eat so do not see.

Along the bottom, blacknose dace
      drag their snouts, suckling the sediment.

Wounded darters
      dive into the mud to hide red markings.
Warpaint shiners
      flash breeding colors, bright enough

to shine through silt. Bluehead chubs continue

to move rocks

  with their mouths. It's harder
  since the banks have eroded,
but they find what they need—

ten thousand stones each.
They build homes of stone.

Inside, the young are born again.

Flourish

Raspberry canes rise up,
bare, sinuous, and, against
the winter field, cold-killed
and colorless—purple.
Bangles clinking at the wrist,
a twist of lemon on a simple dish,
even during this.

Desire

Once, walking in the woods,
I met a hunter.

He spoke. I stopped.
Perhaps I shouldn't have.

But he didn't touch me.
He only

said I moved fast, asked
if I wanted to lead his dogs.

This is not to say
he let me get away.

Ever since, I have dreamed
of running among pointing hounds.

As we slip through the leaves,
the leathery touch of laurel,

the dogs narrow
in the nose and shoulders, grow

into wolves. I go wild too,
and disappear into the trees.

I become why
dogs howl at the forest's edge,

and you wake at night,
and you say, *It's nothing.*

I Learn to Be Still, Like the One I Love

Corn that stood tall
through the flood while houses fell,
that's the kind of thing people like
to talk about. And I had
ambitions. But
there's a drought, and I fell
in love. My love is a hunter.
It's going unnoticed
that he's interested in:
wishing himself away so well,
bears walk past.
He cleans his gun
where hands touch it, because steel
is sensitive to the oils
in human skin.
He works with his rags. I watch,
in silence, since the creek's dried up
and done babbling. I learn
a new aim: leaving no
fingerprints, making no mark.

Epilogue

Old women
who *Set a spell*
on summer evenings,
do make a magic
of slowness,
staring into the woods,
still seeing ginseng
and panthers
in wait among stones.

Acknowledgments

Sincere thanks to the editors of the publications in which some of these poems first appeared:

Alligator Juniper, Annals of Earth, Asheville Poetry Review, The Cortland Review, The Kenyon Review Online, The Laurel Review, New England Review, Orion, Painted Bride Quarterly, Provincetown Arts, The Recorder, Salamander, and *Wilderness.*

Rose McLarney grew up in rural western North Carolina, where she continues to live on an old farm. She teaches at Warren Wilson College, and earned her MFA from the college's MFA Program for Writers. McLarney has been awarded *Alligator Juniper*'s national poetry prize and the Joan Beebe Teaching Fellowship. She was a finalist for the Poetry Foundation's Ruth Lilly Fellowship, and her poems have appeared in *The Kenyon Review, New England Review, Painted Bride Quarterly,* and *Orion,* among other publications.